SEKUNDARSTUFE I

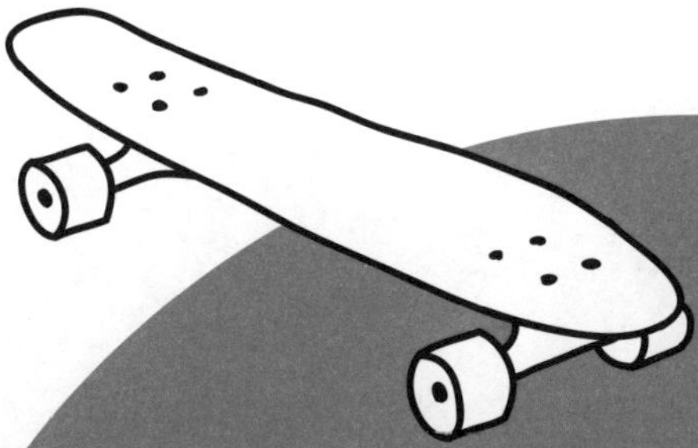

Teen World

Klasse 8–10

Jennifer O'Hagan

Cornelsen

Die Autorin

Jennifer O'Hagan hat Anglistik und Germanistik an der Oxford University studiert. 2013 absolvierte sie ein Volontariat in der Englisch Redaktion des Cornelsen Verlages. Seit 2017 ist sie Lehrerin für Deutsch und Französisch an einer staatlichen Gesamtschule in Cambridge, England.

Projektleitung: Irena Reinhardt und Dorothee Weylandt, Berlin
Redaktion: Barbro Garenfeld, Greven
Umschlagkonzeption/-gestaltung: Corinna Babylon, Berlin
Umschlagabbildungen: shutterstock/Pornprasit (blauer Hintergrund), shutterstock/richardwibi (Herz in Sprechblase), shutterstock/hudhud94 (Smartphone), shutterstock/zizi_mentos (Skateboard), shutterstock/adriano.cz (Britische Flagge)

Layout / technische Umsetzung: LemmeDESIGN, Berlin / Ludger Stallmeister, Wuppertal

www.cornelsen.de

1. Auflage 2019

Druck: H. Heenemann, Berlin

ISBN 978-3-589-16522-3

PEFC
PEFC/04-31-2851

PEFC zertifiziert
Dieses Produkt stammt aus nachhaltig bewirtschafteten Wäldern und kontrollierten Quellen.

www.pefc.de

Inhalt

Einleitung

Beim Thema ‚Teen World' erhalten SchülerInnen die Gelegenheit, über ihre eigene Lebenswelt zu kommunizieren. Darüber hinaus bekommen sie einen Einblick in das Leben ihrer Altersgenossen aus englischsprachigen Ländern. Dieser Austausch zu lebensnahen Fragen und Problemen ist für die Lernenden besonders spannend und motivierend. Zu diesem vielfältigen Thema bietet das Heft verschiedene Ansätze und Zugänge. Somit wird den LehrerInnen und PädagogInnen die Gelegenheit geboten, das Thema ‚Teen World' abwechslungsreich mit der Klasse zu erarbeiten und damit die sprachlichen, landeskundlichen und interkulturellen Kompetenzen der SchülerInnen zu fördern.

Die hier zusammengestellten interessanten Materialien und Inhalte ermöglichen einen zeitgemäßen Blick auf das Thema: Mithilfe von abwechslungsreichen Aktivitäten und authentischen Texten erhalten die Lernenden die Gelegenheit, sich mit einer Reihe von aktuellen Themen wie der wachsenden Bedeutung von Emoticons oder der Rolle des Internets in heutigen Beziehungen zu beschäftigen. Sie können ihre Sprachpraxis verbessern, indem sie über einen Schulausflug ihrer Wahl referieren oder miteinander diskutieren, ob Handys in der Schule verboten werden sollten.

Das Heft besteht aus 26 Kopiervorlagen mit vier Themenbereichen:

- *Interests and activities*
- *Problems and growing up*
- *Youth culture and language* und
- *Love and relationships.*

Jede Kopiervorlage (KV) kann als eigenständige Übung und in beliebiger Reihenfolge als Ergänzung zum gängigen Englischkurs genutzt werden. Bei jeder Übung stehen eine bis zwei Kompetenzen im Fokus: Schreiben, Lesen, Sprechen und/oder Sprachvermittlung. Die jeweiligen Kompetenzen sind aus der Kopfzeile ersichtlich. Übungen, die mit einem ☆ gekennzeichnet sind, gelten als besonders anspruchsvoll (Challenge).

Jennifer O'Hagan

Legende: Symbole

Sprechen	Schreiben	Partnerarbeit
Lesen	☆ Challenge	Gruppenarbeit

I can't live without it!

1 Look at the items below. Which ones are the most important in your life? Write numbers in the boxes. 1 is the most important and 8 is the least important.

Shutterstock/Kenishirotie

Shutterstock/Giuseppe_R

Shutter stock/FocusStocker

Shutterstock/Rauf Aliyev

Shutterstock/ozanuysal

Shutterstock/Roman Sotola

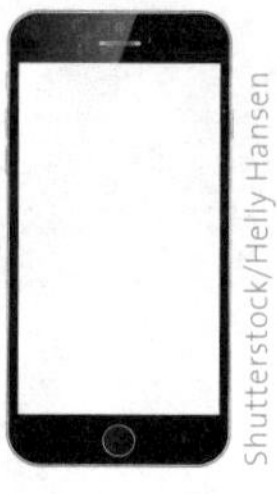
Shutterstock/Helly Hansen

Shutterstock/IB Photography

2 Work with a partner. Discuss your answers.

a) With your partner, try to agree on the three most important things. Use the phrases below to help you.

> I think the ... is/are more important than the ... • I agree/disagree because ... • That's true, but the ... is/are also useful/important ... • I never/always use/wear ... • I could live without (a) ... but not without (a) ... !

b) With your partner, prepare a speech which you will present to the class. Explain to your class which three things are the most important for you. Say why you chose those things.

Autorin: Jennifer O'Hagan: „Teen World", Klasse 8–10

Zack's online profile

Read Zack's description of himself on a social network.

Hi, I'm Zack and I'm 15. My official name is Zachary but only my maths teacher calls me that! My second name is Schneider. I have a German surname because of my dad – he was born in Düsseldorf. I live in Brighton with my family. I have a sister called Hayley, and a cat called Yoyo.

My main interest is music. I have played the guitar for 5 years. I'm also learning to play the keyboard. I'm in a fantastic band called The Ticket Collectors. We are a rock band but we have some quieter songs too. You can find out more about us here ☺.

I am crazy about sports and fitness. I play basketball on Saturdays and I often go running after school. My favourite place to run is along the beach. While I run, I think about music and sometimes I even write songs.

My friends say I am loud and chatty, but I often feel shy with new people.

Shutterstock/Monkey Business Images

© Shutterstock/RemarkEliza

Shutterstock/Mitotico

1 Fill in Zack's profile. You do not need to write in sentences.

- Name: ______
- Age: ______
- Where he lives: ______
- Family: ______
- Pets: ______
- Interests: ______
- Personality: ______

Autorin: Jennifer O'Hagan: „Teen World", Klasse 8–10

ZACK'S ONLINE PROFILE

2 Match the sentence halves. Draw lines.

a Zack's father ...	1 since he was 10.
b Zack's family and friends ...	2 he feels shy.
c He has played the guitar ...	3 at the weekend.
d He plays basketball ...	4 comes from Germany.
e When he goes running ...	5 don't call him Zachary.
f When he is with people he doesn't know ...	6 he thinks about music.

3 a) Now write a text about yourself. Use Zack's text to help you.

____

____

____

____

____

____

b) Work with a partner. Ask him/her to read your text. He/she fills in the profile below about you.

- Name: ______________________
- Age: ______________________
- Where I live: ______________________
- Family: ______________________
- Pets: ______________________
- Interests: ______________________
- Personality: ______________________

Autorin: Jennifer O'Hagan: „Teen World", Klasse 8–10

Do you play an instrument?

1 Find out more about the students in your class and their interests.

a) Choose 6 ideas from the box.

Find someone who ...
- o plays an instrument.
- o likes rock music.
- o often posts photos on social networks.
- o prefers watching sport to playing sport.
- o prefers watching shows online to watching shows on TV.
- o listens to music on the bus/train/tram.
- o likes to read science-fiction books.
- o prefers to read a real book to reading on a tablet.
- o often plays games online.

b) Write your questions in the table. Use the examples to help you.

c) Walk around. Ask questions and fill in your table.

d) ☆ Ask follow-up questions and write this information in your table.

Question	Name	☆ More information
1. *Do you play an instrument?*	*Timo*	*plays the drums – since he was 10*

It's more than a hobby

Do you like exploring incredible places? The Canadian explorer Richard Weber has completed 6 trips to the North Pole. Read the advice he gives in the interview below.

How to prepare for the North Pole

Heading to the northernmost point of the earth – unsurprisingly – isn't as simple as taking the correct equipment and being super fit.

A period of acclimatisation leading up to a trip is necessary, Weber says. "Before going I would head up to somewhere in the Arctic and train for probably about two weeks.

[...] "I've seen people go from Israel straight to the Arctic and you simply can't do that. You have to acclimatise in stages."

No trip is ever the same

Returning to –60° F repeatedly to complete the same challenge might suggest insanity, but Weber insists that no trip to the North Pole is the same, due to the shape-shifting Arctic Ocean.

"One thing about going to the North Pole, is it's always different – especially with climate change. You never know what you're going to get. It's not like climbing a mountain where there's a route and next week it's going to be the same route."

This variation is the main reason for Weber's repeated expeditions, rather than glory. "For me [...] – it's all about the journey, it's not about the goal. I don't do it for the badge. I'm quite satisfied with what I've done, I'm a low key guy, I don't make a big splash about it."

An explorer's diet

When undertaking such an extreme athletic feat, diet is of huge importance. In 1995 Weber and his Russian team-mate Dr Malakhov had to resort to extreme measures.

"During the 1995 expedition we hunted a seal because we were hungry." [...]

However, an Arctic explorer's diet does not usually involve the local wildlife. "You require a high fat diet of about 7,000 calories a day – lots of butter, bacon, macadamia nuts, pecans and freeze dried cheese. My wife designed a recipe for chocolate truffles. Chocolate doesn't have enough calories, but chocolate truffles do. Her recipe manages to pack about 750 calories into 100 grams of chocolate truffles – they're good too."

Source: 'What it´s really like at the North Pole - according an explorer' by Finlay Greig, (https://inews.co.uk/inews-lifestyle/people/secrets-life-polar-explorer-north-pole-richard-weber/), Inewspaper, December 12 2016

Did you know ...?

In 2016 Jade Hameister from Australia became the youngest person ever to ski to the North Pole from an area outside of the Last Degree (about 60 miles). She was only 14 years old at the time!

© Jade Productions Pty Ltd 2018

IT'S MORE THAN A HOBBY

1 Match up the words and phrases from the text with the meanings.

a) equipment	1. getting used to the weather/conditions
b) acclimatisation	2. it plays a big role
c) repeatedly	3. it's different every time you visit
d) no trip is ever the same	4. several times
e) low key	5. need
f) of huge importance	6. quiet; modest; not looking for attention
g) hunted	7. created; made
h) require	8. caught; killed
i) designed	9. things you need to help you complete a task

2 Read the statements and decide if they are true or false.

	T	F
a) Richard Weber comes from Australia.		
b) He did not need to do training before his trip.		
c) Richard Weber has been to the North Pole more than once.		
d) He says that the North Pole is changing because of climate change.		
e) He is not interested in medals and prizes.		
f) It doesn't matter what you eat when you're an explorer.		
g) The chocolate truffles do not taste very nice.		

3 a) Work with a partner. Read the text about Jade Hameister. What questions would you like to ask Jade about her experience? Write at least 3 questions.

____

____

____

____

____

b) Write an e-mail to Jade. Say what you think of her achievement. Ask her some questions. Write your e-mail on a separate piece of paper.

Autorin: Jennifer O'Hagan: „Teen World", Klasse 8–10

Clubs at our school

1 Read adverts for school clubs at Bramble Lane School.

Bramble Blog

Do you have a passion for writing? Are you interested in a career in media? Come and write for our school newspaper. We keep people updated on the most important news in our school. We meet on Mondays at 4pm in Room 8.

Bramble Lane Basketball Club

Are you crazy about basketball? Are you interested in teaching other students how to play? Are you looking for a fun way to do exercise and meet new people? Join our basketball club. We train on Friday lunchtimes in the sports hall. Everybody is welcome!

Drama Club

Drama club is the place to be for all students who have a passion for theatre. You can learn new skills like singing and dancing and take part in fantastic plays and musicals. And you can have a lot of fun! We meet after school on Fridays in the hall.

BLS Charity and Fundraising Club

Do you want to make a difference to peoples' lives? We organise events to raise money for local charities. Our events include: cake sales, sponsored walks, and fancy-dress parties. We meet on Monday lunchtimes in Room 17. See you there!

2 Write the name of at least one club where you can …

a) help other people ____________________

b) take part in shows ____________________

c) stay fit and healthy ____________________

d) sing and dance ____________________

e) write articles ____________________

f) learn about journalism ____________________

g) collect money for charity ____________________

Autorin: Jennifer O'Hagan: „Teen World", Klasse 8–10

CLUBS AT OUR SCHOOL

3 Choose one of the clubs at Bramble Lane School. Imagine you are the president of the club. Write a speech where you persuade other students to join this club. Use the ideas from exercise 2 and your own ideas.

Today I am going to tell you why you should join ______________________.

4 What clubs are there at your school? Write an e-mail to your British penfriend to tell them about the clubs at your school. You could write about:

- popular clubs at your school
- clubs you have joined
- clubs you would like to have at your school

Autorin: Jennifer O'Hagan: „Teen World", Klasse 8–10

What shall we do in Birmingham?

Read about the different things you can see and do in Birmingham, England.

Shutterstock/SilvanBachmann

The **Library of Birmingham** is Europe's biggest public library! There are more than 40,000 books to choose from. You can also chill with friends in the café.

Shutterstock/trabantos

The **Bullring** is easy to find because it is a big silver building. Here you can find all of your favourite shops and cafes. It's a good place to meet friends when it's rainy and cold.

Shutterstock/pixfly

Birmingham is the home of two main **football clubs:** Aston Villa and Birmingham City. You can book a tour of the stadiums or go to see a football match.

Shutterstock/Kris Kuzniar

There are many **canals** in Birmingham. You can take a boat ride through the city. It's also a nice place to just hang out with friends – away from the busy town centre!

WHAT SHALL WE DO IN BIRMINGHAM?

1 Andrew lives in Birmingham and has written about it on his blog. Complete his text using the information from the previous page. Use the words in the box to help you.

city · biggest · hungry · boat trip · canals · football · shopping · quieter · read

Welcome to Birmingham! Birmingham is a large ____________ in the UK. There are lots of things for young people to do here. If you're into ______________, there are two large stadiums you can visit. Or maybe you prefer to go ______________? The Bullring is a great place for that. If you get ____________ there are plenty of restaurants there too. My favourite place to visit is the library. It is huge – in fact it is the ____________ public library in Europe. Sometimes I go there to ____________, and sometimes I go there to meet friends in the café. In the summer I like to hang out near the ____________ with my friends. We like it there because it's ______________ than the city centre. I have never been on a ________________ but I would like to!

2 Work with a partner. Discuss which place(s) in Birmingham you would like to visit. Say why.

3 ☆ Imagine you are organising a class trip to Birmingham. Prepare a presentation for your class to say what you will do on the trip. Use the internet to help you with your research.

Include the following information in your presentation:

- how long you will stay there for;
- where you will stay (hotel / hostel / host families /...);
- what you will visit and why;
- how much it will cost;
- photos of key places.

There's lots to do here!

Create a poster for your British partner school about where you live. Tell them about the different activities young people can do there.

1 Use the mind-map to help you collect your ideas. Write the name of your town/city/ local area in the middle.

Famous sights/buildings

Sports and activities

Places to eat

Things to do on a rainy day

Things to do on a sunny day

2 Now create a poster using the above information. Remember to add pictures and make it look eye-catching.

Autorin: Jennifer O'Hagan: „Teen World", Klasse 8–10

In trouble

Look at the pictures of teens in difficult situations.

Shutterstock/wrangler

Shutterstock/YAKOBCHUK VIACHESLAV

Shutterstock/Monkey Business Images

Shutterstock/Andrey_Popov

1 Choose one of the pictures and describe it. Where is it? What do you think is happening? Discuss your ideas with a partner. Use the phrases below to help you.

- I think he/she/they ... is/are at school/at home/outside
- maybe he/she/they is/are sad/angry/worried because ...
- I agree/disagree because ...
- I think they are arguing because ...
- I think he/she is being bullied
- I think he/she is feeling stressed about ...

IN TROUBLE

2 ☆ Choose a person from one of the photos on page 16. Write a diary entry from his/her perspective. Include the following information:

- what has happened;
- how you are feeling;
- what you hope will happen next.

Autorin: Jennifer O'Hagan: „Teen World", Klasse 8–10

Let's talk about it!

1 Match up the problem with the meaning. Draw lines.

1. Cyberbullying	a) When your friends or people you know make you do things you don't want to do.
2. Peer pressure	b) When people online are mean to you.
3. Exam stress	c) When you are having arguments with your family or the people you live with.
4. Problems at home	d) When you worry about your body or the way you look.
5. Heartbreak	e) When you worry about your school work and your grades.
6. Appearance and self-esteem	f) When romantic relationships end or don't work out.

2 Discuss the list from 1) with a partner.

a) Do you think there are other problems which lots of teenagers have? Add them to the list. Write a meaning or explanation of each problem.

b) What are the two biggest problems for young people? Discuss your ideas.

3 Write an article for your school newspaper about the main problems young people have. Try to include:

- an interesting headline;
- some research or statistics;
- interviews with people in your class.

Write your article on a separate piece of paper.

Exam stress

Read the article about exam stress and how to avoid it.

Exam stress: how to beat it

Stress can sometimes be a good thing as it motivates us to knuckle down and focus on our work. But if stress levels get out of hand because of upcoming exams, this can prevent us from performing our best. Here are some ways you can beat stress and get it under control.

First, you need to know the symptoms. If you've noticed the symptoms below, you may need to address your stress levels. They include:

- Problems with falling asleep or getting up in the morning
- Constant tiredness
- Forgetfulness
- Loss of interest in food
- Loss of interest in activities
- Increased irritability
- Increased pulse
- Migraines/headaches

Here are some ways you can manage the stress:

- Talking! Take a break or talk to someone who knows how you're feeling. This can help you get things back into perspective.
- Try not to compare yourself to other people. There are many ways to revise for exams. You can test different methods and choose the one that works best for you.
- Eat healthily. Have a proper breakfast and eat plenty of fresh fruit and vegetables. Your brain cannot function on just coffee and chocolate.
- Get your eight hours of sleep. Air your room before bed and don't revise under the blanket – your bed is a sanctuary, not a workplace.
- Get moving! Nothing de-stresses the mind faster than physical activity, so build it into your timetable.
- Try not to think about your exams when you have finished them. It's too late to change your answers and it doesn't matter what other people wrote.
- Finally, always remember to breathe! When you feel panicked, take slow, deep breaths.

Autorin: Jennifer O'Hagan: „Teen World", Klasse 8–10

EXAM STRESS

1 Match up the words and phrases from the text with the meanings.

a) to knuckle down	1. to become difficult to control
b) to get out of hand	2. the feeling that you need to sleep
c) to address something	3. to start working
d) tiredness	4. when you easily become annoyed
e) irritability	5. to make comparisons in order to see the situation more clearly
f) to revise	6. a safe place
g) to get things into perspective	7. to act; to do something about it
h) a sanctuary	8. to reread

2 Decide if the following statements are true or false.

	True or false?
a) Stress is always a bad thing.	
b) If you no longer feel hungry, you could be stressed.	
c) All students do revision in the same way.	
d) You should not revise in bed.	
e) Coffee and chocolate will prevent exam stress.	
f) It's helpful to discuss your exams with friends when they are over.	

3 You want to inform students at your school about the symptoms of exam stress. Make a poster in German. Use information from the article.

Autorin: Jennifer O'Hagan: „Teen World", Klasse 8–10

Trouble at school

1 Describe the picture. Use the following question words to help you: who, what, where, why?

Shutterstock/Simone van den Berg

2 a) Work in groups of three. Each person is one of the people from the photo. Create a short role play based on the picture. Use these questions to help you:

- What is the teacher saying to the students? In what kind of tone does he/she speak?
- How do the students respond? Do they respond in different ways?
- How is the situation resolved?

b) Act out the scene in front of the class.

Autorin: Jennifer O'Hagan: „Teen World", Klasse 8–10

TROUBLE AT SCHOOL

3 Do phones have a positive or negative effect on school life? Decide if the ideas below are positive or negative. Fill in the table.

☆ Add your own ideas to the table.

- You can stay in touch with friends and family
- You can easily research things for school work
- Phones can be very distracting
- If your phone makes a noise in a lesson, it distracts other people too
- You can take photos of useful information and you don't need to write it down
- You can easily take/send/post photos of other people at school
- You can easily look up words in other languages
- You can take notes digitally and you save paper
- People use phones instead of actually talking to each other.

positive	**negative**

4 Imagine you are a student at a British school. Write a formal letter to the principal saying:

a) Phones should be banned at school,

or

b) all students should be allowed to use phones at school.

Give reasons. Use the table from 3) to help you.

Autorin: Jennifer O'Hagan: „Teen World", Klasse 8–10

Money trouble

Read the post on a teen online forum.

*Jay*_the*_drums*:*

I'm in serious trouble!! I don't have much money at the moment and I can't find a job in my local town. Last week I saw that my favourite band in the world is playing in London next summer. I knew I had to be there, but the tickets were £60. And I also knew the tickets would sell out very quickly. My mum's bank card was just sitting there on the coffee table in front of me ... so I bought a ticket. I know – it's terrible. It was a moment of madness. I have never done anything like that before.

The thing is, it's been 8 days and my mum has not noticed that the money is gone. Part of me thinks I should not mention it and hope she never notices, and the other part of me thinks I need to tell her! But I am scared she will be so angry and she won't let me go to the concert! Please help me.

1 Put the events in the correct order. The first one has been done for you.

a) He finds out his favourite band will play a concert soon.	
b) Jay uses his mum's card to buy a ticket.	
c) He also worries that he won't be allowed to see the band.	
d) Jay doesn't know if he should tell his mum about using her card.	
e) Jay can't find a job.	1.
f) He worries that soon there will be no tickets left.	

Autorin: Jennifer O'Hagan: „Teen World", Klasse 8–10

MONEY TROUBLE

2 What should Jay do now? Look at the ideas below to decide which is/are the best response(s).

- o Tell his mum what he did – as soon as possible.
- o Tell his mum – but only after the concert.
- o Apologise to his mum and offer to pay her back with money or through chores.
- o Keep quiet and hope that she never notices.
- o Ask for a refund on the concert ticket.
- o Try harder to find a job so that he can give his mum the money.

3. Write an answer to Jay's post. Use the ideas above and your own ideas.

Hi Jay, ______________________

Autorin: Jennifer O'Hagan: „Teen World", Klasse 8–10

Let's debate that!

1 Cut out the statements. Arrange them into two groups: "I agree" and "I disagree."

All teenagers should have a weekend job to prepare them for the future.	Social media should be banned for people under the age of 16.	There should be no exams at school.
Mobile phones should be banned at school.	Young people should be able to vote at the age of 16.	Young people should not have to pay to learn how to drive a car.
The school day should start at 10 a.m.	Teenagers should wear a uniform to school.	It should be illegal to sell unhealthy food to young people.

2 Compare your results with a partner. Are your groups similar or different? Discuss your reasons.

Autorin: Jennifer O'Hagan: „Teen World", Klasse 8–10

LET'S DEBATE THAT!

1 Work in groups of five. Two people are Team A, two people are Team B, and one person is the moderator. Choose one of the cards from the previous page.

a) Team A: You are going to **disagree** with this statement. Make notes on your reasons.

b) Team B: You are going to **agree** with this statement. Make notes on your reasons.

c) Carry out the debate. The moderator introduces the topic and makes sure that each person has a chance to speak.

Autorin: Jennifer O'Hagan: „Teen World", Klasse 8–10

What's your style?

Look at the pictures below.

1
Shutterstock/Kent Weakley

2
Shutterstock/Anna Om

3
Shutterstock/Shvets Anna

5
Shutterstock/ASDF_MEDIA

6
Shutterstock/Christopher Gardiner

4
Shutterstock/Alexander Supertramp

8
Shutterstock/Cookie Studio

7
Shutterstock/Africa Studio

9
Shutterstock/MJTH

Autorin: Jennifer O'Hagan: „Teen World", Klasse 8–10

WHAT'S YOUR STYLE?

1 Play the game below with a partner. After each round, swap roles. The winner is the person who is fastest to guess the correct photo.

Partner A: Choose one of the people in the photos on page 27. Don't tell Partner B which person you have chosen. You can only answer 'yes' or 'no' to questions from Partner B.

Partner B: Ask questions in order to find out who Partner A has chosen. Use the box below to help you. Remember, Partner A can only answer with 'yes' or 'no.'

- Is he/she wearing a hat/t-shirt/jumper/jeans/trainers/...?
- Is he/she outside/inside/on the sofa/...?
- Is he/she fashionable/creative/sporty/chilled/ ...?
- Does he/she look happy/sad/cool/silly/nice/...?

2 Choose one of the photos on page 27. Write a description of the person in the picture. Include the following points:

- his/her outfit or style;
- what kinds of interests you think the person has;
- if you like his/her style;
- if it is different or similar to your style.

Autorin: Jennifer O'Hagan: „Teen World", Klasse 8–10

Sharing, posting, commenting

1 Complete the sentences about digital communication. Use the words in the box. For some gaps there is more than one word you could use.

a) If you want to tell your friends what you did today, you can __________ a status update or __________ a photo.

b) If you think something is cool and you want other people to see it, you can __________ it.

c) If you think something is cool you can also click "__________"!

d) If you *really* like something, you can post a __________.

e) If you want to listen to a song or podcast, you can sometimes ______________ it.

f) If you're a musician, you can ____________ videos of your band for other people to see.

g) If you want to share your opinion of something online, you can write a ____________.

h) If you think something is funny, you can write __________. It means "laughing out loud."

i) If you don't want to use words and letters, you can say many things just with ______________.

emoticons • upload • comment • write • LOL • ♥ • download • like • share • post

2 Write about how you communicated online yesterday. Use the phrases above to help you.

____

____

____

____

____

____

____

____

____

____

____

Autorin: Jennifer O'Hagan: „Teen World", Klasse 8–10

Class survey: How often do you post photos?

1 How do people in your class communicate online? Do a survey in your class. Use the table on the next page. Ask as many people as you can. Put a tick in the correct box for each person.

2 Write a text about your results. Use the phrases below to help you.

Some/most people in our class send e-mails / post photos a few times per week.
Only one person in our class ...
About half of the people in our class ...

Autorin: Jennifer O'Hagan: „Teen World", Klasse 8–10

CLASS SURVEY: HOW OFTEN DO YOU POST PHOTOS?

How often do you ...	More than once a day	A few times per week	A few times per month	Never
... send e-mails?				
... send messages or 'chat' online?				
... post photos?				
... share articles/ videos with others?				
... upload videos?				
... use emojis? ☺ ☹				
... write comments, for example about articles you read online?				
... read other peoples' comments online?				
... download podcasts?				

Social Media: spending your time and money on it?

Read the article about how young people are using social media in the UK.

Forty percent of millennials 'can't live' without social media' and a fifth blame it for lack of savings

Four in 10 millennials 'can't live' without social media.

Researchers polled 2,000 UK adults aged 15 to 24 and found they are increasingly dependent on the likes of Facebook, Twitter and Instagram and couldn't bear to be away from it.

On average they'll check up on the latest posts from friends, family and big-name celebs 30 times a day.

Draining our time

The Royal Society for Public Health (RSPH) called on young people to cut down their social media usage – with thousands expected to take part in 'Scroll Free September'.

The research – which was commissioned by Barclays – found social media left a dent in our pockets as well as drained our time. More than half have purchased items endorsed by celebrities or influencers on social media, while one fifth directly blame it for a lack of savings.

Fifty-three per cent believe their bank balances would be in a much better shape if wasn't for tempting posts in their social media feeds. Young Brits think they would have £398.76 more in their savings accounts on average – that's a huge £3 billion collectively.

Who has responsibility?

As a result, 52% of those polled would like celebs and other big-name social media influencers to provide more advice and support on how to save money. In an effort to change online spending habits, lifestyle blogger, Jasmine Cecilia Jonas, joined their campaign and said: "It's very easy to flick through an influencer's feed and see a 'dream lifestyle' that you wish to lead too, but many people don't realise that the majority of clothes, holidays and experiences displayed have actually been given as gifts."

[...]

Source: 'Forty percent of millenials "can´t live without social media" and a fifth blame it for lack of savings' by iTeam, (https://inews.co.uk/culture/millenials-social-media-spending-habits-savings-tips/), INewspaper, September 5th 2018

SOCIAL MEDIA: SPENDING YOUR TIME AND MONEY ON IT?

1 Match up the words and phrases from the text with the meanings.

a) millennials	1. to leave you with less money
b) polled	2. most of
c) big-name celebs	3. to do something less often
d) to cut down on something	4. young adults in today's society
e) to leave a dent in your pocket (fig.)	5. bought
f) purchased	6. famous people
g) the majority of	7. surveyed; asked

2 Decide if the following statements are true or false.

	True or false?
a) All millennials are dependent on social media.	
b) In 'Scroll Free September', people will try to use social media less often.	
c) Many people buy products which they have seen on social media.	
d) Young British people do not think social media has an impact on their finances.	
e) More than half of the young people would like to have more financial advice from influencers.	
f) Jasmine Cecilia Jonas says the 'dream lifestyle' is not very expensive for the influencers.	

3 ☆ Do you think that young people spend too much money because of advertising on social media? Why/why not?

____

____

____

____

____

____

Autorin: Jennifer O'Hagan: „Teen World", Klasse 8–10

Our own language

Look at the photos below.

Shutterstock/ pikcha

Shutterstock/ Mego studio

1 Work with a partner. One person chooses a picture. He/she describes it to the partner. Then swap roles. Include the following details in your description:

- what is happening in the picture;
- how you think the person is feeling;
- if you like the picture;
- your opinion of emojis.

2 Can you communicate just with emojis? Try to 'write' the below sentences using only emojis or pictures. Compare your emojis with a partner. Who has presented the meaning of the sentences the best?

- That's so funny!

____

- I can't believe it!

____

- I'm waiting for you.

____

- Love you!

____

- That's so annoying.

____

- I'm so tired today, and have so much homework to do!

____

- I'll bring the cake and some cola.

____

- Happy birthday! Have a great time in Spain!

____

A positive message

Read the text about how young celebrities are using social media.

Cyberbullying is undoubtedly still a huge problem. However, more and more celebrities are using their popularity to spread more positivity and to oppose haters.

Imago Stock & People GmbH/ZUMA Press

Millie Bobby Brown, who is mostly known for her performance as Eleven on the Netflix series *Stranger Things*, has created a new Twitter account called @MillieStopsHate. Millie describes the purpose of her new account as following: *"I want this account to share love and positivity. Let's stop bullying."* Millie uses the account to give advice to young people who are experiencing bullying. Today, this account has gained more than 250,000 followers. Clearly there are many people who share Milly's wish for more positivity.

Another actress who uses social media as a force for good is Emma Watson, who is famous for many roles including the role of Hermione in the Harry Potter films. She uses her social media accounts to raise awareness of different charities and to show support for people who are fighting inequality across the world. Today she has nearly 30 million followers on Twitter. It seems that her positive vibes are very popular.

Autorin: Jennifer O'Hagan: „Teen World", Klasse 8–10

A POSITIVE MESSAGE

1 Match up the words and phrases from the text with the meanings.

a) to oppose haters	1. received; attracted
b) gained	2. helpful tips and information
c) to wish for	3. when some people don't have the same rights as others
d) a force for good	4. to want sth. very much
e) advice	5. to fight against hatred
f) raise awareness	6. to help people to learn about something
g) inequality	7. a way to improve the world

2 Match up the sentence beginnings with the correct ending.

a) Cyberbullying is still ...	1. different charities.
b) Millie Bobby Brown is ...	2. people who are fighting against inequality.
c) She made a new account on social media because ...	3. a famous actress.
d) Emma Watson supports ...	4. she wanted to share positivity and stop bullying.
e) She also helps her followers find out about ...	5. a major problem.

3 What do you think of Millie's idea? Write a short message to let her know.

Autorin: Jennifer O'Hagan: „Teen World", Klasse 8–10

Our online campaign

1 Work in groups of four. What could you do to create a positive impact online? Use the mind map below to collect your ideas. Write your goal in the middle.

2 Present your ideas to the class.

Who is our target audience? (young people in this country / people all over the world / ...)

Do we want to raise money? How?

Our goal is ...

Research: what do we need to find out before we start?

Will we use social media platforms? How? (posting photos / sharing news articles / ...)

Autorin: Jennifer O'Hagan: „Teen World", Klasse 8–10

My perfect partner

1 Which characteristics are important in a boyfriend or girlfriend? Find the correct word for each definition. Use the words in the box.

a) ____________________: he/she always tells the truth and doesn't lie.

b) ____________________: he/she believes in him/herself and doesn't care what other people think.

c) ____________________: he/she is funny and makes you laugh.

d) ____________________: he/she is attractive.

e) ____________________: he/she spends money on you and gives you presents.

f) ____________________: he/she does cute things like organise a surprise picnic.

generosity • confidence • humour • honesty • romance • good-looking

2 ☆ Which other characteristics are important in a partner? Add three more qualities to the list. Give definitions.

____

____

____

3 a) Which characteristics are the most important for you? Give the qualities in a–f a number from 1–8. 1 = most important, 8 = least important.

____

____

____

____

____

____

____

____

b) Describe what is important for you in a partner. Use the phrases below to help you. Write your answer on a separate piece of paper.

In my opinion the most important quality is • ... is also important because ... • ... is not so important for me. • the least important quality is ... because ...

Autorin: Jennifer O'Hagan: „Teen World", Klasse 8–10

A really bad date

Read the posts on a teen online forum. The teens are writing about their worst date.

Ally126:	Mine was last summer. I didn't have much money and neither did my date. We wanted to do something cheap, so we went to the park. It started to rain as soon as we got there. We had no alternative plan so we both just went home. The date lasted 15 minutes in total!
*Jo**:*	I was 14. It was my first date and I was so nervous. The problem is when I am nervous I never stop talking! I talked non-stop for about an hour. I didn't find out anything about my date!
Sammy_Sunshine:	I am loving these posts. I have never been on a date but I feel less nervous after reading these posts.
Number1_Alex:	Mine was a couple of years ago. I was crazy about this girl from school. We wanted to meet up in town but my mum said I was too young to go out on my own. So the girl came around to my house to watch TV. My mum sat with us the whole time. It was so awkward. We didn't hang out again after that ☹
Jane♥:	I'm not sure if you can call it a date. It was in the school canteen. I gathered all my courage and decided to go and sit next to this guy I liked. I thought that would be easier than asking him to go on a date. It wasn't! Every single person in the canteen seemed to notice! People made so many stupid comments to us! I was so embarrassed. Luckily, he was pretty cool about it ☺

Autorin: Jennifer O'Hagan: „Teen World", Klasse 8–10

A REALLY BAD DATE

1 Write the correct name/username in the gaps.

a) ____________________'s date took place at school.

b) ____________________ was not allowed to go on a date in town.

c) ____________________ now feels less nervous about dating.

d) ____________________'s date was ruined by the weather.

e) ____________________ didn't give his/her date the chance to speak.

f) ____________________ had a very short date.

2 Find words in the text which mean the same as:

a) not expensive ____________________

b) worried/anxious ____________________

c) without pausing ____________________

d) two years ago ____________________

e) uncomfortable ____________________

f) fortunately ____________________

3 ☆ Write your own post for the forum. It can be about something which really happened or it can be completely made-up!

____

____

____

____

____

____

____

____

____

____

____

Autorin: Jennifer O'Hagan: „Teen World", Klasse 8–10

Love stories

Love stories are often a main theme in books and films. What makes them good?

1 Make notes about your favourite love story. It could be from a film / book / TV show / comic. It doesn't need to be a 'romantic' film, it could also be a sub-plot in an action or sci-fi film. Use the mind map to help you collect ideas.

2 Present your ideas to the class.

Things which would make the love story better.

What is the name of the film/ book where the story happens?

My favourite love story is ...

Why this love story stands out for you. What makes it good?

Description of the key characters.

Autorin: Jennifer O'Hagan: „Teen World", Klasse 8–10

A difficult situation

Read the post below from a teen forum.

So here is the situation. I have been with my girlfriend for 8 months and it's been amazing. We are in the same class at school so we see each other most days. She is funny, clever, and really cool. She gets on well with all of my friends. She makes me sooo happy.

But a week ago she told me her family is moving to Newcastle. I can't believe it. I have no idea what to do. Newcastle is about 4 hours away by train. I don't know if I will have the time or money to see her.

She says that we can make it work and tells me not to worry. She says that even though we will see each other less often, we can still speak every day on the phone. But I am seriously worried! Is there any point in staying together? It seems so difficult ☹

I'd love to hear what you guys think of this. I am so confused right now.

Anonymous_16

Shutterstock/ Phoenixns

Autorin: Jennifer O'Hagan: „Teen World", Klasse 8–10

A DIFFICULT SITUATION

1 Decide if the statements below are true or false.

	T	F
a) The relationship began 2 years ago.		
b) The writer's friends do not like his girlfriend.		
c) The writer feels happy with his girlfriend.		
d) He is not surprised that she is moving away.		
e) The girlfriend is not worried about the future.		
f) The writer is worried about the future.		

2 What should Anonymous_16 do now? Look at the ideas below and decide which is/are the best response(s).

- o Stay together and see how it goes – it might be easier than you think.
- o Tell your girlfriend how you are feeling.
- o Talk to your parents, maybe they can help.
- o End the relationship now while you are still happy.

3 ☆ Write an answer to Anonymous_16's post. Use the ideas above and your own ideas.

Hi Anonymous_16, ______________________________

____

____

____

____

____

____

____

____

Autorin: Jennifer O'Hagan: „Teen World", Klasse 8–10

Relationships: public or personal?

Read the article about Twilight star Kristen Stewart.

For years, Kristen Stewart resolutely tried to keep her private life out of the public eye.

Now, though, the actress says that she has decided to share her relationship experiences with the world as an opportunity to "make even one other person feel good about themselves".

Stewart was in a long-term relationship with her Twilight co-star Robert Pattinson but the couple broke up in 2013. Then last year, Stewart came out as gay.

In an interview with The Sunday Times, the 26-year-old, who stars in Olivier Assayas's latest film Personal Shopper, a ghost story set in Paris, said: "I wasn't hiding anything [...] I didn't talk about my first relationships that went public because I wanted things that are mine to be mine.

"I hated it that details of my life were being turned into a commodity and peddled around the world.

"But considering I had so many eyes on me, I suddenly realised [that my private life] affects a greater number of people than just me. It was an opportunity to surrender a bit of what was mine, to make even one other person feel good about themselves."

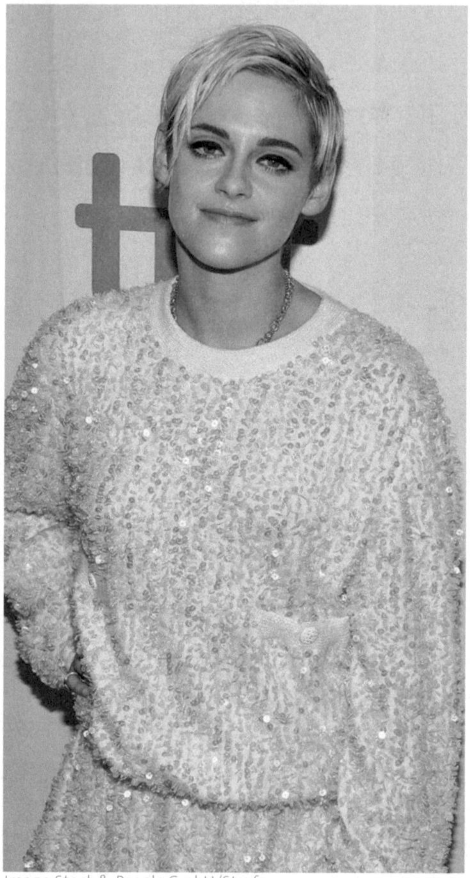

Imago Stock & People GmbH/Starface

"If it didn't seem like a relevant topic [...] like something that needed help," she said, "I would have kept my life private for ever. But then I can't walk outside holding somebody's hand, as I'm followed everywhere.

"When I was dating Rob, the public were the enemy – and that is no way to live. It wasn't this grand statement, 'I was so confused! Now I've realised who I am!' I have not been struggling [...] It just seemed important, and topical."

[...]

Source: Kristen Stewart on opening up about her sexuality: 'My private life affects a greater number of people than just me', Rupert Hawksley, Telegraph Media Group Limited 2017)

Autorin: Jennifer O'Hagan: „Teen World", Klasse 8–10

RELATIONSHIPS: PUBLIC OR PERSONAL?

1 Match up the words and phrases from the text with the meanings.

a) For years, Kristen Stewart resolutely tried to keep her private life out of the public eye.	1. the public treated me badly
b) the couple broke up	2. Many people knew about me / were interested in me
c) turned into a commodity and peddled around the world	3. For a long time, she tried to keep her private life private.
d) I had so many eyes on me	4. something which can be bought and sold everywhere
e) the public were the enemy	5. they separated

2 Match up the sentence beginnings with the correct ending.

a) In the past ...	1. ... to be like a product.
b) She used to date ...	2. ... could help other people.
c) She didn't want her private life ...	3. ... her former co-star Robert Pattinson.
d) More recently, she announced ...	4. ... Kristen Stewart wanted to keep her relationships private.
e) She decided that information about her private life ...	5. ... she is gay.

3 ☆ Discuss the following statement with a partner: "I suddenly realised [that my private life] affects a greater number of people than just me." What does Kristen Stewart mean? Summarise your discussion. Write two sentences.

____

____

____

____

____

____

Autorin: Jennifer O'Hagan: „Teen World", Klasse 8–10

Relationship debates

1 Work in groups of four. Discuss each point for 4–5 minutes. Collect arguments for and against each point.

"Relationships should be a private thing, not a public thing."	"Online dating should be banned for teenagers."
"Love stories are boring."	"Online communication makes relationships easier."

Autorin: Jennifer O'Hagan: „Teen World", Klasse 8–10

RELATIONSHIP DEBATES

2 Now choose one statement that you find interesting. Write a text about it. Use the ideas from your group work to help you. Include the following points:

- arguments for and against the statement;
- your own opinion;
- examples from the media or from your own experiences;
- research quotes or statistics to support your points.

Autorin: Jennifer O'Hagan: „Teen World", Klasse 8–10

Lösungen

Interests and activities

KV 1 Individuelle Lösungen.
KV 2 **1** Zachary Schneider, 15, Brighton (UK), parents and sister, a cat (Yoyo), music/sports/fitness, loud/chatty/sometimes shy; **2** a-4, b-5, c-1, d-3, e-6, f-2; **3** Individuelle Lösungen.
KV 3 Individuelle Lösungen.
KV 4 **1** a-9, b-1, c-4, d-3, e-6, f-2, g-8, h-5, i-7; **2** a-f, b-f, c-t, d-t, e-t, f-f, g-f; **3** Individuelle Lösungen.
KV 5 **2** a BLS Charity and Fundraising Club, b Drama club, c Bramble Lane Basketball Club, d Drama club, e Bramble Blog, f Bramble Blog, g BLS Charity and Fundraising Club; **3 & 4** Individuelle Lösungen.
KV 6 **1** city, football, shopping, hungry, biggest, read, canals, quieter, boat trip; **2 & 3** Individuelle Lösungen.
KV 7 Individuelle Lösungen.

Problems and growing up

KV 8 Individuelle Lösungen.
KV 9 **1** 1-b, 2-a, 3-e, 4-c, 5-f, 6-d, **2 & 3** Individuelle Lösungen.
KV 10 **1** a-3, b-1, c-7, d-2, e-4, f-8, g-5, h-6; **2** a-f, b-t, c-f, d-t, e-f, f-f; **3** Individuelle Lösungen.
KV 11 **1–4** Individuelle Lösungen.
KV 12 e-1, a-2, f-3, b-4, d-5, c-6, **2 & 3** Individuelle Lösungen.
KV 13 Individuelle Lösungen.

Youth culture and language

KV 14 **1 & 2** Individuelle Lösungen.
KV 15 **1** a write, post, b share, c like, d ♥, e download, f upload, g comment, h LOL, i emoticons; **2** Individuelle Lösungen.
KV 16 Individuelle Lösungen.
KV 17 **1** a-4, b-7, c-6, d-3, e-1, f-5, g-2; **2** a-f, b-t, c-t, d-f, e-t, f-t; **3** Individuelle Lösungen.
KV 18 Individuelle Lösungen.
KV 19 **1** a-5, b-1, c-4, d-7, e-2, f-6, g-3; **2** a-5, b-3, c-4, d-2, e-1; **3** Individuelle Lösungen.
KV 20 Individuelle Lösungen.

Love and relationships

KV 21 **1** a honesty, b confidence, c humour, d good-looking, e generosity, f romance; **2 & 3** Individuelle Lösungen.
KV 22 **1** a Jade, b Number1_Alex, c Sammy_Sunshine, d Ally126, e Jo**, f Ally126; **2** a cheap, b nervous, c non-stop, d a couple of years ago, e awkward, f luckily; **3** Individuelle Lösungen.
KV 23 Individuelle Lösungen.
KV 24 **1** a-f, b-f, c-t, d-f, e-t, f-t; **2 & 3** Individuelle Lösungen.
KV 25 **1** a-3, b-5, c-4, d-2, e-1; **2** a-4, b-3, c-1, d-5, e-2; **3** Individuelle Lösungen.
KV 26 **1 & 2** Individuelle Lösungen.

Autorin: Jennifer O'Hagan: „Teen World", Klasse 8–10